FREEDOM SEEKING

A Complementary Workbook to Freedom Seeker

Revised Edition

Tiffani Harvey

Written Words Publishing LLC
14189 E Dickinson Drive, Unit F
Aurora, Colorado 80014
www.writtenwordspublishing.com

Freedom Seeking © 2015 by Tiffani Harvey
Revised Edition

All rights reserved. No part of this publication may be reproduced, stored in a retrieval system, or transmitted in any form by any means, electronic, mechanical, photocopying, recording, or otherwise, without the prior permission of the author.

Published by Written Words Publishing LLC 9/16/2020

ISBN: 978-1-7332357-6-1 (paperback)
ISBN: 978-1-7332357-7-8 (eBook)

Library of Congress Control Number: 2020915236

Cover Designed by Written Words Publishing LLC

Manufactured and printed in the United States of America

Reviews

"These books were written to help disabled people function in this complicated world. It's hard enough for the able bodied to do, sometimes. So, you can imagine how more difficult it can be for the disabled. Whether they have someone to help them function or on their own, Tiffani's books can help. She has listed a lot of agencies or places that can assist the disabled population, to help them function in society. Things to stay away from and ideas to help them stay safe. She makes it easy to find the topic that interests you. She also has a workbook, so you can record your progress." Judy S. and Del S.

"Tiffani has written a simply useful guideline to [let] those who have disabilities know that they are not alone when making important decisions on their welfare. Congratulations on sharing these steps with those who seek out your wisdom." Beverly J.

"The author takes the reader on an in depth journey of her life and the not so easy choices. She mentions resources that better the lives of the disabled." Esther, Former President of SASP

"Tiffani has covered many topics and she has very helpful information. She also has a workbook. She is very positive and confident. You almost forget that she has restrictions. Read her book and you'll be blessed and you can help others." Gloria P.

"My family is so happy with books. My 10 and 12 year old says these books have answers to various questions in life and they guide someone in making right choices since it talks about disadvantages of various questions and how to deal with them. They love these books." Daudeti from Uganda

Table of Contents

Acknowledgements vii
Forward viii
Introduction 1
Protecting Yourself 2
Personal Information 4
Medications 12
Personal Preferences 18
All Safety Issues 20
Communication/Conversation Opinions 21
Personal Safety 27
Stranger Questions in General 33
Gossiping (Conversation Do Nots) 35
Home and Neighborhood Safety 38
Protecting Yourself from Stalking and Violence When Dating, Married or Living Together 42
Internet Safety 57
Learning How to Manage Your Money 59
General Money Safety 66
Financial Safety 68
Addictions 70
Alcohol 71
Smoking 74
Local Transportation 78
Disability Van 80
City Bus 82
Driving 84

Employment 87
How to Narrow Down Your Choice of Jobs 93
College 95
Wants 98
    Choosing a Cell Phone Company 98
    Cell Phone Prices 99
    Your Job Might Limit Your Choices! 101
Out of Town Traveling 106
Looking for a Close Relationship 116
Raising Children 120
Resources for the Disability Community 127
The Challenges of Living on Your Own 132
Is Guardianship Good or Bad? 135
Notes 137
About the Author 140

Acknowledgements

This workbook was made possible because of Greg Falk, former CEO of The Arc of Spokane. I would like to take this opportunity to thank Greg for his insight in *A Journey to Independence*. He said, "You ask a lot of questions, but you left no space for people to write the answers." I was too far along to go back and add the needed spaces, so I just started from scratch and made this workbook to go along with my story or to work as a stand-alone!

Forward

Freedom Seeking is a book of questions for the reader to use as a guide, with a little information, definitions, and examples. The reader is encouraged to come up with their own questions and decide if the questions the author suggests are good questions for them to ask.

This book has some ideas and a few personal opinions of the author. The reader has the choice to agree or disagree with some or all of the book.

The reader is responsible for their own choices and behaviors in relation to application and use of the book's content. The author does not claim responsibility, liability, loss, or risk, directly or indirectly.

Introduction

Freedom Seeking is a workbook to let your doctors, family, caregivers, guardians, and others know what your likes and dislikes are. This workbook gives you the chance to tell others why you like and dislike different things.

It covers many subjects from who your professionals are to what your values are such as religious, political, cultural, etc. This workbook covers entertainment and habits to the way you like to communicate with others and more, such as the way you handle your money, etc.

You will be asked questions to clarify that the answers really are _yours_. The reason: To help _you_ know yourself better and to help your personal and professional support teams protect you and your values.

In my opinion, it's easier to support and help someone when you understand why someone likes or dislikes things. It's also nice to know how much a person likes or dislikes things.

For example, "Do you want cable TV?"

"No."

"Why, why not, etc.?"

"Watching TV is a waste of time and money."

If someone calls and asks, "Will you support us politically?" My answer is, "I don't know."

"Why, etc.?"

"I need to know who they are and what kind of support they are asking for? If they need money, how will it be spent?"

Finally, know your priorities. This is important, so if you have religious, family, employment, or college responsibilities at the same time, you will know what to do first, second, third, etc. For example, it is against some people's religion to work on a certain day of the week, depending on their particular religion.

Protecting Yourself

Here's a list of terms and simple definitions:

"Wise," being wise, wisdom (in the context of this book) means what you have learned from knowledge and experience.

"Good choices" are choices that keep you healthy and/or safe, but you might not understand why or how those choices keep you healthy or safe. (For example, you may choose not to smoke, but you may not know or understand the risks.)

"Knowledge" means having the facts in your head.

"Gaining knowledge" means the process of getting this knowledge. We can have knowledge without experience. (For example, you should know to *never* touch a hot stove even if you've never touched one.)

"Understanding" means comprehending what the consequences of your choices are, whether they are good or bad.

It is important to listen to other people and find out what other people say on any subject or every subject. Find out if it's a fact or opinion. The way to tell if something is a fact or opinion is to ask, "Where did you get your information from?" If the person cannot tell you, it's probably an opinion. Keep an open mind. Find out how many people have that opinion and why. When possible, find some facts before you make a choice about anything!

To know the difference between fact and opinion, take what is said with a grain of salt. If lots of people say the same thing, it's probably worth looking into as a fact or a smart opinion for consideration.

For example, pregnant women drinking—some people may tell you their religious or moral beliefs or opinions, and other people may tell you their medical knowledge, and some people may think drinking is okay as long as a woman is not pregnant, etc.

Develop your own opinions on every topic and be open to logic and reason. *Be willing to change your opinion **when someone gives you reasons to change** your mind on any subject!*

"Experience" means the knowledge gained by having done something in the past. For example: At age 10, I saw two $1 lottery tickets on the ground. My mom asked me, "Do you want to buy two more lottery tickets, or do you want me to cash in the $2 and give it to you?" This was my mom's way of teaching me a lesson about gambling so I would stop looking at the fast, easy money and take the time to observe!

Do you think we won any more money or lost the $2 we bought the tickets with? We lost the $2 and we didn't buy anymore! *That was my _experience_ with gambling!

"Foolish" means making bad choices because you didn't ask anyone with knowledge or experience, or you refused to listen to what others had to say. A foolish person refuses to ask for advice from someone who has the knowledge, understanding, and experience to help them gain knowledge and understanding such as, "What does someone need to know and understand to be and stay safe?"

"Bad choice" is often a foolish choice. It's made when you don't understand ALL the results of the choice you made.

"Wrong choice" means choosing to do something that is against the law and/or choosing to do something that hurts others or you so badly that someone dies or can't recover. Making choices that others would consider foolish or bad are okay _if you learn_ from your mistakes and the mistakes of others; it will help you become wiser.

If no one ever makes a mistake, they will never gain experience or learn from their mistakes!

Personal Information

Name: _____

Date: _____

Address: _____

_____

Date of Birth: _____

Day Phone: _____

Evening Phone: _____

Cell Phone: _____

Email: _____

Your support team: _____

_____

    Your support team can be anyone you trust. Remember, there are personal and professional support teams.

    (Most of the time, I will use "substitute decision maker" no matter which kind of surrogate decision maker I'm talking about. The reason: There are several kinds of "substitute decision makers," but since I'm not a lawyer, I leave it up to you, the reader, to get legal advice. This is not a legal book!)

Who are your family members and friends you want to help you make decisions?

_____

_____

Do you want to give your opinions to another person and have that person make the final choice? (Check one.)

    ___ Yes   ___ No

Who do you want to make the final decisions over your everyday choices in life if you cannot or do not want to speak for yourself? (List in order who you want these people to be.) If you don't know, who are the people you trust most? Narrow it down to the three people you trust most. Number them in order.

1. _____

2. _____

3. _____

If you don't know the names, addresses or phone numbers of any of the professionals that I am going to ask you in following questions, leave the space blank. Where it asks for your power of attorney (POA) or guardian and alternates/standby guardian, specify what their job title is.

Power of Attorney

Name: _____

Job Title: _____

Address: _____

_____

Phone: _____

Email: _____

Guardian

Name: _____

Job Title: _____

Address: _____

_____

Phone: _____

Email: _____

Alternative POA #1

Name: _____

Job Title: _____

Address: _____

_____

Phone: _____

Email: _____

Alternative POA #2

Name: _____

Job Title: _____

Address: _____

_____

Phone: _____

Email: _____

Advocate

Name: _____

Address: _____

_____

Phone: _____

Email: _____

Advocate

Name: _____

Address: _____

_____

Phone: _____

Email: _____

Doctor M.D.

Name: _____

Address: _____

_____

Phone: _____

Email: _____

Dentist

Name: _____

Address: _____

_____

Phone: _____

Email: _____

Eye Doctor

Name: _____

Address: _____

_____

Phone: _____

Email: _____

Special Doctor

Name: _____

Address: _____

_____

Phone: _____

Email: _____

Special Doctor

Name: _____

Address: _____

_____

Phone: _____

Email: _____

Special Doctor

Name: _____

Address: _____

_____

Phone: _____

Email: _____

Social Worker

Name: _____

Address: _____

_____

Phone: _____

Email: _____

Social Worker

Name: _____

Address: _____

_____

Phone: _____

Email: _____

Care Giving Agency

Name: _____

Address: _____

_____

Phone: _____

Email: _____

Case Manager

Name: _____

Address: _____

_____

Phone: _____

Email: _____

Other Professional

Name: _____

Address: _____

_____

Phone: _____

Email: _____

On the lines, write what kind of power of attorney or guardian you have. If you have an alternate power of attorney or a standby guardian, write it on the lines.

_____

_____

_____

_____

_____

_____

_____

Medications

Your health is important to those who personally know you because they want the best for you. Your health is important to me because I strive for everyone's freedom and independence. Taxpayers care about health. The healthier people are, the lower healthcare taxes are. To those who love you, it's important because they know you. I care about your health because it's important for people to know themselves.

If medicine can help, why avoid it? It's supposed to make you as healthy as possible!

"Informed consent" is a paper you sign after a doctor or nurse explains all the possible benefits and risks and what you should expect from what they give you, such as medicine or surgery. ***Don't sign anything you don't understand!***

Here are a few questions to ask your doctor if you don't know the answers. If you know the answer, write it down, but don't ask your doctor.

How is each medicine supposed to help you?

_____

_____

_____

Is each one of your medicines doing what it is supposed to for you?

___ Yes ___ No ___ Some of Them ___ Don't Know

How?

_____

_____

How does the medicine you take benefit you?

_____

_____

_____

What side effects are you suffering and what medicine is causing it?

_____

_____

_____

What side effects are you willing to suffer?

_____

_____

_____

Find out if your doctor has any other ideas of how to manage your medical/mental health problem other than prescription medicine.

What are other ways you can think of to manage your medical/mental health along with taking prescription medicine?

_____

_____

_____

Do you know what could happen to you if you don't take prescription medicine? Ask your doctor or pharmacist if you don't know.

    ___ Yes ___ No ___ Kind Of

If you don't want to take medicine, will you:

Eat healthy?

    ___ Yes ___ No ___ Think About It

Take vitamins?

    ___ Yes ___ No ___ Think About It

Get counseling?

    ___ Yes ___ No ___ Think About It

Exercise often?

    ___ Yes ___ No ___ Think About It

Avoid foods that could increase the reason for taking medicine?

    ___ Yes ___ No ___ Think About It

Eat foods that could reduce the reason for taking the medicine?

    ___ Yes ___ No ___ Think About It

The following questions tell others what you want to be able to do yourself, what you need/want to learn so you can do it yourself, and what you need/want others to do for you.

Do you want to take *your own* medicine and vitamins?

    ___ Yes ___ No ___ Maybe
    ___ Need to Learn at Another Time

Do you want to make a plan to help you remember to take your medicines, vitamins, etc. every day?

___ Yes ___ No ___ Maybe ___ Don't Know

If yes, what's your plan? If maybe or don't know, what information do you need to find before making a decision?

_____

_____

_____

_____

Do you want to make a plan to let yourself know when you have already taken your medicines, vitamins, etc. so you won't accidently take too much medicine?

___ Yes ___ No

Do you want to make a plan to take the correct medicines, vitamins, etc. at the correct time of day?

___ Yes ___ No ___ Maybe ___ Don't Know

If yes, what's the plan? If maybe or don't know, what information do you need to find out to make an informed choice?

_____

_____

_____

_____

If you have medicines with different instructions for day and night, would you be able to always remember those instructions?

    ___ Yes   ___ No

How do you plan on finding a trusted person to teach you how to take your medicines correctly?

_____

_____

_____

If you don't know who you want to teach you, what do you need to find out to make that decision?

_____

_____

_____

Who do you want to give you your medicines?

_____

If you don't know, what do you need to find out to make that decision?

_____

_____

_____

How do you want to get information from your pharmacy?

    ___ By Myself   ___ Someone Else   ___ Don't Know

If someone else, who?

_____

If you don't know, what do you need to find out to make that decision?

_____

_____

_____

Do you want to talk to your medical team or do you want someone else to do it? (These could be signing papers such as a release of information, "informed consent" papers, etc.)

___ You   ___ Someone Else   ___ Don't Know

If someone else, who?

_____

Why did you choose that person (even if it's you)? If you don't know, what do you need to find out to make that decision?

_____

_____

_____

Personal Preferences

Do consider yourself to be religious?

___ Yes ___ No ___ Maybe ___ Don't Know

If yes, what is your faith/religion?

_____

Why did you choose that faith/religion?

_____

_____

_____

If no, are you looking for a faith/religion, a place of worship, or are you open to anyone talking to you about their faith/religion or where they attend worship services?

___ Yes ___ No ___ Maybe ___ Don't Know

Why or why not?_____

_____

_____

Are you registered to vote?

___ Yes ___ No ___ Don't Know

Being a registered voter does not mean you have to vote! It means you have the choice to vote each time there is an election. If you are not registered to vote, you don't have the option. You cannot vote *before* you are registered!

If you are not registered to vote, do you want to be registered to vote?

___ Yes   ___ No   ___ Maybe   ___ Don't Know

Why or why not?_____

_____

_____

All Safety Issues
What Is Your Comfort Zone?
What Do You Feel Comfortable With?

For these next few statements, what would you do? Are you comfortable:

    Being alone? ___ Yes ___ No

    Being in a group? ___ Yes ___ No

Does it change depending on the situation?

___ Yes ___ No

When you are new to a group are you:

    Comfortable watching others for the first few times?

    ___ Yes ___ No

    Comfortable jumping into a conversation when it's your first time?

    ___ Yes ___ No

    Are you both ways, depending on the group you are in?

    ___ Yes ___ No

    Does it depend on the situation?

    ___ Yes ___ No

Communication/Conversation Opinions

What people say, their tone of voice, facial expression and body language can make others feel comfortable or uncomfortable. The same is true about what is not said.

What is your opinion of another person doing most of the talking and not letting you speak very much?

_____

_____

_____

_____

_____

Do you like to talk nonstop and not allow the other person to talk very much?

___ Yes   ___ No   ___ Sometimes

What would you do if someone does not respond to you when you say, "Hi," "Hello," or "How are you?"

_____

_____

_____

_____

_____

Safe and Unsafe Conversations

How would you approach someone you want to talk to? What are things you could say?

_____

_____

_____

_____

How do you get the attention of a person who has a visual impairment if you don't know their name and you want to talk to them?

_____

_____

_____

If you are shopping in the grocery store and someone bumps into you saying, "Oh, I'm sorry," is it appropriate for you to give them your name?

    ___ Yes   ___ No   ___ Sometimes
    ___ Maybe   ___ Don't Know

Why or why not?_____

_____

_____

_____

When you ask or someone else asks you, "How are you," should one of you share a little about yourself and then should the other person share a little about themselves?

___ Yes ___ No ___ Sometimes
___ Maybe ___ Don't Know

Why or why not?_____

_____

_____

_____

What do you consider to be safe topics? (Check all that apply.)

___ Food ___ Music ___ Sports ___ Religion
___ Weather ___ School ___ Employment
___ Politics ___ Other

Is it okay to ask a stranger, "How are you," if their body language is friendly?

___ Yes ___ No ___ Sometimes
___ Maybe ___ Don't Know

Why or why not?_____

_____

_____

_____

What do you consider to be unsafe topics of conversation? (Check all that apply.)

___ Food ___ Music ___ Sports ___ Religion
___ Weather ___ School ___ Employment
___ Politics ___ Other

Why do you consider these unsafe subjects/topics?

_____

_____

_____

_____

If someone makes a rude comment about someone with a disability, what should you do? (Check all that apply.)

___ Educate them

___ Just walk away

___ Leave the choice up to the person who has the disability (if the comment is directed at someone)

___ Ignore the comment 100% and keep talking to them as if you didn't hear what they said

If you choose to stop and educate that person, would you take the person's feelings into consideration?

___ Yes ___ No ___ Sometimes ___ It Depends
___ Maybe ___ Don't Know

Why or why not?_____

_____

_____

_____

When meeting someone new, are there subjects that you don't want to talk about?

___ Yes ___ No ___ Maybe ___ Don't Know

Why or why not?_____

_____

_____

If you answered yes, what are those subjects?

_____

_____

Do you think the person you are meeting has subjects they don't want to talk about?

___ Yes ___ No ___ Maybe ___ Don't Know

Why or why not?_____

_____

_____

How would you like people making comments about your looks, speech, or the way you walk, etc., if it was because of your disability?

___ Like it ___ Dislike it ___ Not Sure ___ Don't Know

Why or why not?_____

_____

_____

Do you think it is right to make comments about the color of someone's skin?

___ Yes ___ No ___ Sometimes
___ Maybe ___ Don't Know

Why or why not?_____

_____

_____

Do you think it is okay to make comments about someone's gender? Gender means male or female.

    ___ Yes   ___ No   ___ Sometimes
    ___ Maybe   ___ Don't Know

Why or why not?_____

_____

_____

Do you think it is okay to make comments about someone's age?

    ___ Yes   ___ No   ___ Sometimes
    ___ Maybe   ___ Don't Know

Why or why not?_____

_____

_____

Personal Safety

When you are out in the public, knowing what to do and where to go if someone wants to hurt you is *very important*! It is important to have a plan before any possible problems come up!

The following ideas are put into the form of questions. Consider these ideas as ways to protect yourself! If you have any other ideas for staying safe, do those things and share them with others. (Please email your ideas to me at responsiblyindependent@yahoo.com.)

Do you want to take a self-defense class where they help you use your weaknesses or disabilities as an asset instead of a barrier?

___ Yes   ___ No   ___ Maybe   ___ Don't Know

Why or why not?_____

_____

_____

_____

Do you need a cell phone for emergency purposes only?

___ Yes   ___ No

Why or why not?_____

_____

_____

_____

Name three reasons why you would call 911 on your cell phone.

1. _____

2. _____

3. _____

Do you want a cell phone for other safety reasons and other reasons?

   ___ Yes ___ No

If yes, what are those reasons? _____

_____

_____

_____

If no, why not? _____

_____

_____

_____

Do you think that you should talk to your support team or an advocate about other safety issues?

   ___ Yes ___ No

Why or why not?_____

_____

_____

_____

Name three safety reasons for owning a cell phone other than calling 911.

1. _____

2. _____

3. _____

If someone was following you or was doing something you told them to stop doing, would you report them to the police?

    ___ Yes   ___ No   ___ Maybe   ___ Don't Know

Why or why not?_____

_____

_____

If you choose to make a police report, you need to know the date, the time, and give as many specific details as possible.

Do you know *what* mace, pepper spray, or a zapper is used for? Answer Yes or No for each of the following:

    Mace: ___ Yes ___ No

    What is mace? _____

    _____

    Pepper spray: ___ Yes ___ No

    What is pepper spray? _____

    _____

Zapper: ___ Yes ___ No

What is a zapper? _____
_____

Do you know *when* you are supposed to use each one of these devices?

Mace: ___ Yes ___ No

When? _____
_____

Pepper spray: ___ Yes ___ No

When? _____
_____

Zapper: ___ Yes ___ No

When? _____
_____

Do you know *how* to use each one of the following devices? Answer yes or no for each.

Mace: ___ Yes ___ No

How? _____
_____

Pepper Spray: ___ Yes ___ No

How? _____
_____

Zapper: ___ Yes ___ No

How? _____

_____

Think about doing any or all of the following suggestions to "act safe" even when you "feel unsafe," so you can "*stay safe.*"

Would you walk with your head held high as if you know where you are going even if you are lost?

    ___ Yes   ___ No   ___ Sometimes
    ___ Maybe   ___ Don't Know

Why or why not?_____

_____

_____

Would you walk a little faster even if you were just hanging out or in a hurry?

    ___ Yes   ___ No   ___ Sometimes
    ___ Maybe   ___ Don't Know

Why or why not?_____

_____

_____

Would you walk fast if you thought you were in danger?

    ___ Yes   ___ No   ___ Sometimes
    ___ Maybe   ___ Don't Know

Why or why not?_____

_____

_____

Would you want to look like you are walking with a specific place to go and as if you need to get there quickly (even if you don't)?

    ___ Yes   ___ No   ___ Sometimes
    ___ Maybe   ___ Don't Know

Why or why not?_____

_____

_____

Do you think the suggestions listed above, would help you be safer, not as safe, or equally as safe as you are now?

    ___ Safer   ___ Not As Safe
    ___ Equally As Safe As You Are Now

Explain your opinion.

_____

_____

_____

_____

_____

Stranger Questions in General

Would you feel comfortable getting advice from a stranger?

    ___ Yes   ___ No   ___ Sometimes
    ___ Maybe   ___ Don't Know

Why or why not? _____

_____

_____

Do you think it is appropriate to give advice to a stranger?

    ___ Yes   ___ No   ___ Sometimes
    ___ Maybe   ___ Don't Know

Why or why not? _____

_____

_____

Do you think a stranger would feel comfortable getting advice from someone they don't know?

    ___ Yes   ___ No   ___ Sometimes
    ___ Maybe   ___ Don't Know

Why or why not? _____

_____

_____

If a stranger comes up to you and asks you to do a favor for them, would you do it?

    ___ Yes   ___ No   ___ Sometimes
    ___ Maybe   ___ Don't Know

Why or why not?_____

_____

_____

Would you go up to a stranger and ask them to do you a favor?

    ___ Yes   ___ No   ___ Sometimes
    ___ Maybe   ___ Don't Know

Why or why not?_____

_____

_____

Gossiping (Conversation Do Nots)

Gossiping is talking about someone who is not included in the conversation.

Are you or someone around you gossiping?

___ Yes ___ No

A good test would be to ask yourself, "Would I say it if they were listening?" Answer this question silently to yourself.

___ Yes ___ No ___ Maybe ___ Don't Know

If the answer is no, it is gossiping. If the answer is yes, it is not gossiping.

Here are two situations. Consider each situation and decide if it is gossiping?

Two college students were talking and one student said, "I work in the student government."

The other student said, "Oh, then you must know Angel."

The first student thought for a while and finally said, "So many students come through the office I can't remember her."

The second student gave some very specific physical descriptions of her, and the first student remembered who she was. "Oh yeah, she's real nice. She keeps us on our toes and fights for the disabled!"

The second student said, "That's my wife!"

Do you think that man would mind if the husband told his wife?

___ Yes ___ No ___ Maybe ___ Don't Know

Explain: _____

_____

_____

How do you think Angel felt when she heard it?

_____

_____

_____

A second example is, someone says, "She would look so much more professional and beautiful if she would just stop body piercing and putting tattoos all over herself! She looks like garbage!"

How would you feel if she heard you saying that and saw you pointing at her?

___ Embarrassed   ___ Ashamed   ___ Angry
Other _____   Other _____

Why do you feel that way?

_____

_____

_____

How would you feel if someone talks about you when you are not there?

_____

_____

_____

If someone you know is gossiping to you about someone else, chances are that person is going to gossip about you to another person, maybe even to your friends.

Give four examples of gossiping to show that you understand what gossiping is.

1. _____

2. _____

3. _____

4. _____

If you found out a friend was gossiping to you about another friend, what would you do?

_____

_____

_____

_____

_____

Home and Neighborhood Safety

When you leave home, do you lock the doors and windows?

___ Yes ___ No

Why or why not?_____

_____

_____

_____

When you go to bed, do you lock the doors and windows?

___ Yes ___ No

Why or why not?_____

_____

_____

_____

    Timers on lights mean the lights are timed to turn on and off in different rooms in your home. As one light goes off, another light turns on a couple of seconds after the other light turned off.

Do you want to get timers on your lights?

___ Yes ___ No ___ Maybe ___ Don't Know

Why or why not?_____

_____

_____

_____

If you are buying or own your home, this next question is especially for you:

Would you get a security alarm for your home?

    ___ Yes   ___ No   ___ Maybe   ___ Don't Know

Why or why not?_____

_____

_____

_____

When walking down the street, would you walk against the traffic or with the traffic?

    ___ With   ___ Against   ___ Doesn't Matter to You
    ___ Don't Know

Why?_____

_____

_____

_____

When riding a bicycle down the street, would you ride with or against the traffic?

    ___ With   ___ Against   ___ Doesn't Matter to You
    ___ Don't Know

Why?_____

_____

_____

_____

Driving Strangers or Riding with Strangers Safety

Do you know what hitchhiking is?

    ___ Yes   ___ No   ___ Kind Of

What is hitchhiking?

_____

_____

_____

What is your opinion of hitchhiking?

    ___ Approve   ___ Disapprove   __ Not Sure
    ___ Don't Know

Why or why not?_____

_____

_____

Would you accept a ride from a stranger?

    ___ Yes   ___ No   ___ Sometimes
    ___ Maybe   ___ Don't Know

Why or why not, or under what circumstances?

_____

_____

_____

Would you offer a ride to a stranger?

    ___ Yes   ___ No   ___ Sometimes
    ___ Maybe   ___ Don't Know

Why or why not, or under what circumstances?

_____

_____

_____

Would you feel safe riding alone with a stranger?

    ___ Yes   ___ No   ___ Sometimes
    ___ Maybe   ___ Don't Know

Why or why not, or under what circumstances?

_____

_____

_____

Would you feel comfortable giving a ride to a stranger?

    ___ Yes   ___ No   ___ Sometimes
    ___ Maybe   ___ Don't Know

Why or why not, or under what circumstances?

_____

_____

_____

Protecting Yourself from Stalking and Violence When Dating, Married or Living Together

The reason for writing the following story is to get you thinking about **where** you feel safe or unsafe meeting someone you would consider dating, living with, or marrying.

Basically, how long would you want to know someone in public before you exchange different kinds of personal information?

I never considered finding a spouse on public transportation, but that's how I met my husband. One day, I saw a boy in a wheelchair sitting in my favorite spot on the bus. I chose to sit in front of him, introduced myself, and started talking to him. His caregiver spoke up and helped him communicate. The boy was unable to speak. I kept running into the same boy and the same caregiver. Finally, I asked the caregiver two questions: "Don't you ever get a day off?" and "Why can't you remember my name?"

The answers were, "I'm not his caregiver. I'm his father. I'm blind. I can't see who is talking to me."

The father and I enjoyed the same kind of music, we both rode the city bus, and we also had similar hobbies. Finally, I heard the boy at my church and went searching for him and his father. Our employment goals, some of our hobbies, and some of our political views were different, but we were able to accept each other's differences.

Talk to your support team about safety measures. Safety measures would be: How long do you want to know someone before you allow them in your space or before you give out your personal information? Know the kind of personalities you get along with and the ones you can't deal with. *Know yourself* well enough to answer the following questions, and if you can't answer all the questions, it would be smart to save dating, living together and marriage for later in the future.

Know yourself well enough to set your own boundaries. Know yourself well enough to know what *your* safety boundaries are. Safety boundaries include space and touch boundaries. If the two of you like enough of the same things to make a friendship into a special relationship, then the two of you need to establish what kind of relationship you have.

To check them out for safety, make a lot of copies of the following checklist and go through the checklist for each person you would consider having a close friendship with.

First of all, did you meet someone you would like to have a closer friendship with?

___ Yes ___ No

If yes, who?_____

For each person, go through the safety checklist:

Have they put you down with words?

___ Yes ___ No ___ Maybe ___ Don't Know

If yes, what have they said?

_____

_____

_____

Do you know if they have put others down with words?

___ Yes ___ No ___ Maybe ___ Don't Know

Do they limit the friends you can have?

___ Yes ___ No ___ Sometimes ___ Don't Know

If you don't know, what steps will you take to find out if they limit who you can have as friends?

_____

_____

_____

_____

Under what situations do they limit or control how much contact you have with your family or friends?

_____

_____

_____

_____

Do they tell you when you can or can't go out?

    ___ Yes ___ No ___ Don't Know

How often?

    ___ Never ___ Rarely ___ Sometimes
    ___ Often ___ Always

Do they tell you when you have to be home?

    ___ Yes ___ No ___ Don't Know

How often?

    ___ Never   ___ Rarely   ___ Sometimes
    ___ Often   ___ Always

Do they tell you what time you are allowed to go out and what time to be home?

    ___ Yes   ___ No   ___ Don't Know

How often?

    ___ Never   ___ Rarely   ___ Sometimes
    ___ Often   ___ Always

Do they tell you where you can or can't go?

    ___ Yes   ___ No   ___ Don't Know

How often?

    ___ Never   ___ Rarely   ___ Sometimes
    ___ Often   ___ Always

Do they tell you who you can or can't call?

    ___ Yes   ___ No   ___ Don't Know

How often?

    ___ Never   ___ Rarely   ___ Sometimes
    ___ Often   ___ Always

Do they tell you for what reason(s) you can or can't go out?

    ___ Yes   ___ No   ___ Don't Know

How often?

    ___ Never   ___ Rarely   ___ Sometimes
    ___ Often   ___ Always

Do you ever feel unsafe with this person?

    ___ Yes ___ No ___ Maybe ___ Don't Know

How often?

    ___ Never ___ Rarely ___ Sometimes
    ___ Often ___ Always

Have they ever controlled anyone else that you know of?

    ___ Yes ___ No ___ Kind Of ___ Not Sure
    ___ Don't Know

Do they take your money without your permission?

    ___ Yes ___ No ___ Don't Know

How often?

    ___ Never ___ Rarely ___ Sometimes
    ___ Often ___ Always

Have they taken anyone else's money without them knowing?

    ___ Yes ___ No ___ Maybe ___ Don't Know

How often do they try to make you feel guilty on purpose?

    ___ Daily ___ Weekly ___ Biweekly
    ___ Monthly ___ Yearly

How often have they tried to make others feel guilty on purpose?

    ___ Daily ___ Weekly ___ Biweekly
    ___ Monthly ___ Yearly

Are they jealous of your time, energy or possessions?

    ___ Yes ___ No ___ Sometimes
    ___ Maybe ___ Don't Know

Has this person ever been jealous of anyone else's time, energy or possessions?

    ___ Yes ___ No ___ Sometimes
    ___ Maybe ___ Don't Know

Has the person that you want to date or marry ever made you feel uncomfortable by trying to get information you don't want to share when they called and wanted to know what you were doing?

    ___ Yes ___ No ___ Don't Know

How often?

    ___ Never ___ Rarely ___ Sometimes
    ___ Often ___ Always

(It's great to set boundaries, but it's up to every person how much information they want to share.)

Have they ever isolated you?

    ___ Yes ___ No ___ Don't Know
    ___ Never ___ Rarely ___ Sometimes ___ Always

If yes, do you think it would be smart to break off contact?

    ___ Yes ___ No

Do you know if they have ever isolated others?

    ___ Yes ___ No ___ Don't Know

How often?

    ___ Never ___ Rarely ___ Sometimes
    ___ Often ___ Always

Do they have a history of physically abusing animals?

    ___ Yes ___ No ___ Maybe ___ Don't Know

If you answered "maybe" or "don't know," how would you find out?

_____

_____

_____

Do they have a history of sexually abusing animals?

___ Yes ___ No ___ Maybe ___ Don't Know

If you answered "maybe" or "don't know," how would you find out?

_____

_____

_____

Do they have a history of physically abusing children?

___ Yes ___ No ___ Maybe ___ Don't Know

If you answered "maybe" or "don't know," how would you find out?

_____

_____

_____

Do they have a history of sexually abusing children?

___ Yes ___ No ___ Maybe ___ Don't Know

If you answered "maybe" or "don't know," how would you find out?

_____

_____

_____

If the answer is "yes," "maybe," or "don't know" to any of the physical or sexual abuse questions, why would you want to be friends with, date, and/or marry that person?

_____

_____

_____

_____

_____

Have they destroyed your stuff?

___ Yes ___ No ___ Maybe ___ Don't Know

Do you know if they have ever destroyed anyone else's stuff?

___ Yes ___ No ___ Maybe ___ Don't Know

Some people argue all the time, others hate arguing. Some people are the peacemakers, and others like to cause trouble.

Do you like to be around peacemakers?

___ Yes ___ No ___ Doesn't Matter ___ Don't Know

Do you like to be around troublemakers?

___ Yes ___ No ___ Doesn't Matter ___ Don't Know

Do you like the kind of people who stir the waters by fighting for good causes?

    ___ Yes   ___ No   ___ Doesn't Matter   ___ Don't Know

Do you like to be a peacemaker?

    ___ Yes   ___ No   ___ Doesn't Matter   ___ Don't Know

Do you like people with compassion?

    ___ Yes   ___ No   ___ Doesn't Matter   ___ Don't Know

Does the volume of someone's voice matter to you?

    ___ Yes   ___ No   ___ Sometimes
    ___ Depends on the Situation   ___ Don't Know

If sometimes, when does volume bother you?

_____

_____

_____

Did you grow up with arguing all around you?

    ___ Yes   ___ No

Do you like constant arguing?

    ___ Yes   ___ No   ___ Maybe   ___ Don't Know

Why or why not?_____

_____

_____

Do you like to argue?

    ___ Yes   ___ No   ___ Sometimes

How often?

___ Rarely ___ Sometimes ___ Often ___ Always

If arguing is a habit, would you like to break the habit or continue to argue with them?

___ Yes ___ No ___ Maybe ___ Don't Know

Do you want to continue arguing in future relationships?

___ Yes ___ No ___ Maybe ___ Don't Know

Why or why not?_____

_____

_____

Do they hold grudges?

___ Yes ___ No ___ Sometimes ___ Don't Know

Do they make you feel guilty when you hurt their feelings or do they forgive you?

___ Guilty ___ Forgiving ___ Don't Know

Do you hold grudges against them or forgive them?

___ Grudges ___ Forgiving ___ Don't Know

Do you make others feel guilty when your feelings get hurt?

___ Yes ___ No ___ Sometimes ___ Don't Know

Which kind of people do you like being around? (Check all that apply.)

___ A passive person
___ An assertive person
___ An aggressive person
___ A passive-aggressive person

Regarding the question above, everyone who cares about you should know why you choose to be like that. This should be *out of concern*, not control!

(I would want to get this information from my teenage son/daughter even if they don't have disabilities. If I knew nothing else about who my adult children were dating or going to marry, I would want to know why they were interested in the different types of people listed above.)

Do you like being around people who are sensitive to you?

___ Yes ___ No ___ Sometimes ___ Don't Know

Do you like being around people who are sensitive to others?

___ Yes ___ No ___ Sometimes ___ Don't Know

Do you like being around people who have a military-style personality?

___ Yes ___ No ___ Sometimes ___ Don't Know

If you are not sure about any of the above set of questions, what do you need to find out to decide?

_____

_____

_____

_____

Do the two of you share the same spiritual background?

___ Yes ___ No ___ Maybe ___ Don't Know

If not, does the other person respect your spiritual background or lack of?

___ Yes ___ No ___ Maybe ___ Don't Know

If not, why? _____

_____

_____

_____

Do you respect the other person's spiritual background or lack of?

    ___ Yes ___ No ___ Maybe ___ Don't Know

If not, why? _____

_____

_____

_____

If you have the same spiritual background, what have they written, said or done that made you believe they are telling the truth?

_____

_____

_____

_____

Do the two of you share the same political views?

    ___ Yes ___ No ___ Maybe ___ Don't Know

If not, does the other person respect your political viewpoints or lack of?

    ___ Yes ___ No ___ Maybe ___ Don't Know

Do you respect the other person's political viewpoints or lack of?

___ Yes ___ No ___ Maybe ___ Don't Know

If not, why? _____

_____

_____

Does the other person respect your choice for a career or a job?

___ Yes ___ No ___ Maybe ___ Don't Know

If not, why? _____

_____

_____

Do you respect the other person's choice for a career or a job?

___ Yes ___ No ___ Maybe ___ Don't Know

Why or why not, or what do you need to find out to make an opinion about their career?

_____

_____

_____

_____

If you are going to go to college, does the other person emotionally support or encourage you with your educational goals?

    ___ Yes   ___ No   ___ Maybe   ___ Don't Know

If the other person is going to college, are you emotionally supporting or encouraging the other person's educational goals?

    ___ Yes   ___ No   ___ Maybe   ___ Don't Know

Why or why not?_____

_____

_____

_____

Is the other person afraid for your health and/or safety?

    ___ Yes   ___ No   ___ Sometimes
    ___ Maybe   ___ Don't Know

If so, what exactly is the other person scared about and why?

_____

_____

_____

_____

Are you afraid of the other person's health and/or safety?

    ___ Yes   ___ No   ___ Sometimes
    ___ Maybe   ___ Don't Know

If so, why are you concerned about the other person's health and/or safety?

_____

_____

_____

_____

Internet Safety

Regarding the internet, be very careful when you write to people you've *never* met *in person*! Protect your personal information.

The reason is, anyone can send a fake picture. They can be a criminal who says they are a priest and they may be a truthful person, but the problem is, <u>*you just don't know*</u>. It's better to stay safe instead of taking a risk by possibly putting yourself in danger!

Bad things happened in 2006 with myspace.com. Myspace.com was supposed to be for teenagers *only*. Some criminally minded adults got into myspace.com to find teenagers for sexual purposes.

It's your choice who you choose to talk to on the internet. **Be very careful!**

Think very <u>***carefully***</u> about dating someone you met over the internet! ***Create and set internet boundaries for meeting anyone you met over the internet.*** Your boundaries for people you date on the internet <u>*should be stricter*</u> than for people you meet in person.

(I suggest that you don't date anyone you meet on the internet. If you were my kid or close friend, I'd discourage you from dating anyone you meet through the internet.)

How long would you want to be writing back and forth over the internet before you feel safe talking to this person on the phone?

_____

_____

_____

What is everything *you* need or want to know about this person before talking to them on the phone?

_____

_____

_____

_____

How long would you want to talk to them on the phone before meeting them face-to-face?

___ Weeks   ___ Months   ___ Years

What is everything you need and want to know about this person over the phone before meeting them face-to-face?

_____

_____

_____

_____

Learning How to Manage Your Money

Do you want to manage your own money?

    ___ Yes   ___ No   ___ Don't Know

Why or why not?_____

_____

_____

_____

Do you need to learn how to manage your money?

    ___ Yes   ___ No   ___ Maybe   ___ Don't Know

Do you want to learn how to manage your money?

    ___ Yes   ___ No   ___ Maybe   ___ Don't Know

If you need or want to learn to budget your money, check all the people or agencies that you would trust to teach you money management skills:

    ___ Family
    ___ Friends
    ___ Your religious organization(s)
    ___ Social service organization/Non-profit organization
    ___ Others

What are the names of those people or organization(s)?

_____

_____

_____

A representative protective payee is only allowed to manage a person's government money. If you have an inheritance, life insurance, wages, or any other money coming in, a representative protective payee is not allowed to manage it. A trustee can handle all types of money no matter where it comes from. It can include stocks, bonds or insurance payments also.

Do you have a trustee?

    ___ Yes   ___ No   ___ Don't Know

If you want to know about stocks, bonds or trusts, ask your family, trustee, social service or financial agencies, or substitute decision maker.

Do you want a protective payee?

    ___ Yes   ___ No   ___ Maybe   ___ Don't Know

Why or why not?_____

_____

_____

Who do you want your payee to be? (A protective payee can work for many customers.)

_____

_____

This next section of three sets of questions has to do with what your beliefs are as far as giving money.

Do you believe in giving money to religious organizations?

    ___ Yes   ___ No   ___ Sometimes   ___ Maybe
    ___ Not Sure   ___ Don't Know

Why or why not?_____

_____

_____

_____

How much money a week, a month, a year, or every pay period would you want to give to a religious organization? (This could change as the amount of your income changes.)

_____

_____

Do you believe in giving money to non-profit organizations?

    ___ Yes   ___ No   ___ Sometimes
    ___ Maybe   ___ Don't Know

If so, who?_____

_____

_____

How much money a week, a month, a year, or every pay period would you want to give to a non-profit organization? (This may change as the amount of your income changes.)

_____

_____

Do you believe in giving money to political candidates?

    ___ Yes   ___ No   ___ Sometimes
    ___ Maybe   ___ Don't Know

Why or why not? _____

_____

_____

_____

How much money a week, a month, a year, or every pay period would you consider giving to a candidate or cause? (This may change as the amount of your income changes.)

_____

_____

These next questions are to help you to know some of your boundaries, to know when others are financially hurting you and what your financial choices are!

What religious/spiritual causes would you consider giving part of your money to?

_____

_____

_____

What non-profit organizations would you consider giving part of your money to?

_____

_____

_____

What political causes would you consider giving part of your money to?

_____

_____

_____

These next questions ask what business you want to hold your money and what types of accounts you want to have.

Do you want to have your money in a credit union, a bank, or both?

    ___ Credit Union   ___ Bank   ___ Both   ___ Don't Know

Which one and why?_____

_____

_____

Do you want a savings or checking account or both?

    ___ Savings   ___ Checking   ___ Both   ___ Don't Know

Why?_____

_____

_____

How do you want to pay your bills? Do you want to pay by: (Check all ways that are acceptable to you.)

    ___ Money order
    ___ Checking account
    ___ Pay your bills online
    ___ Automatic bill payment
    ___ Debit Card

Why do you like these ways of paying?

_____

_____

_____

_____

Do you want to carry cash on hand?

___ Yes ___ No ___ Sometimes
___ Maybe ___ Don't Know

Why or why not? _____

_____

_____

_____

Do you know what a credit card is?

___ Yes ___ No ___ Don't Know

What is it? _____

_____

_____

_____

Do you want a credit card(s)?

___ Yes ___ No ___ Maybe ___ Don't Know

If so, how many? _____

Why that many credit cards?

_____

_____

_____

Do you know what a debit card is?

___ Yes   ___ No   ___ Don't Know

Explain it. _____

_____

_____

Do you want a debit card(s)?

___ Yes   ___ No   ___ Maybe   ___ Don't Know

If so, how many? _____

Why that many debit cards?

_____

_____

_____

General Money Safety

Would you feel safe if someone asked you, "How much money do you make?"

___ Yes ___ No ___ Maybe ___ Don't Know

If so, who?_____

_____

Do you think another employee would feel comfortable around you if you asked them, "How much money do you make?"

___ Yes ___ No ___ Maybe ___ Don't Know

Why or why not? _____

_____

_____

_____

Would you feel comfortable telling your friends how much money you make?

___ Yes ___ No

If so, why?_____

_____

_____

_____

Is it smart to lend money to others?

___ Yes ___ No ___ Depends on the Situation
___ Depends on Who It Is ___ Don't Know

If it depends on the situation, what would your guidelines be and who would *you* feel safe lending your money to?

_____

_____

_____

_____

Would you ever consider asking for money from others or does it depend on the situation?

    ___ Yes ___ No ___ Depends on the Situation
    ___ Don't Know

Why or why not, or under what circumstances would you say it's okay to ask someone for money?

_____

_____

_____

_____

Financial Safety

Who would you give your bank account number to?

_____

_____

Why would you give your bank account number to those people?

_____

_____

_____

Who would you give your Social Security number to?

_____

_____

Why would you give your Social Security number to those people?

_____

_____

_____

Who are the people you would give your bank account and Social Security information to?

_____

_____

Why would you give your bank account number and your Social Security number to those people?

_____

_____

_____

Would you want to talk to your support team before giving personal information to important people?

　　___ Yes ___ No

Why or why not?_____

_____

_____

Who are the people your support team says can have your bank account and Social Security numbers?

_____

_____

Addictions

People who drink alcohol and smoke usually socialize, date, or marry people who drink and smoke; however, nonsmokers usually won't allow smoking in their home or car. Knowing why you smoke and drink or don't will help you stick to your boundaries.

For example, as a nonsmoker, this one person visits with recovering alcoholics *on the phone* as long as they do not start drinking again. She will get together with them in public, but her smoking friends don't smoke in her home, and she doesn't go to theirs. She will visit with smokers outside while they are smoking. She has her own reasons for associating with recovering friends and smoking friends from a distant!

Once you find out that something is "unsafe," "dangerous," or "unhealthy," think about avoiding those things. For example, if anyone in your professional or personal support team tells you that smoking, drinking, taking illegal drugs, or gambling are unhealthy, unsafe, dangerous, or risky, *think about* avoiding people who practice risky behaviors. If you need or want to find out why they are saying it is safe or unsafe, etc., it is reasonable to ask. Remember, you chose the people you want to help you when you don't know what questions to ask or choices to make.

If you choose to make a different choice than your support team, tell them why and what your protection barriers are.

Do your research and talk it over with several trusted people.

Alcohol

Before making any choices about drinking alcohol get information from all the resources you can find! You can call the Prevention Center at (509) 922-8383.

Talk to all your doctors and your pharmacy who know your personal medical and mental health history! It is your choice if you take someone with you or go alone.

As a woman, consider if you want to get pregnant in the future. (These next questions are for you to ask your doctor.)

Will alcohol have any negative effects on a child if you get pregnant?

___ Yes ___ No ___ Maybe ___ Don't Know
___ Does Not Apply

If the answer is yes or maybe, ask your doctor what the possible negative effects could be.

_____

_____

_____

Will the baby outgrow any of those negative effects?

_____

If you drink while pregnant, your baby could have developmental disabilities, mental health problems or physical disabilities! The more a woman drinks and/or takes illegal and prescription drugs while she is pregnant, the higher the risk that the child could be born with severe disabilities! I personally know ten adults with severe disabilities who must have someone around them, 24 hours a day, seven days a week!

Who could you give your keys to if you want to drink at a party?

_____

Who do you need and want to talk to about making the choice of who you would feel safe giving your keys to temporarily until you are sober?

_____

Do you still want to drink alcohol?

___ Yes   ___ No   ___ Sometimes   ___ Don't Know

Why or why not?_____

_____

_____

If you choose to drink, what are the health and safety barriers you would put in place (i.e., giving car keys to a friend until you sober up)?

_____

_____

_____

If you choose not to drink, why?

_____

_____

_____

If sometimes, in what situations is it okay to drink and in what situations is it not okay to drink?

_____

_____

_____

_____

_____

Do you know what a "recovering alcoholic" is?

___ Yes ___ No

Are you a recovering alcoholic?

___ Yes ___ No

Smoking

Are you a smoker?

    ___ Yes ___ No

Do you enjoy smoking?

    ___ Yes ___ No ___ Sometimes
    ___ Never Thought About It

Why or why not? _____

_____

_____

If you smoke, do you want to quit?

    ___ Yes ___ No ___ Sometimes
    ___ Maybe ___ Don't Know

Why or why not? _____

_____

_____

If you are currently a smoker, have you tried to quit smoking, and started smoking again?

    ___ Yes ___ No

    If you are a smoker and want to continue smoking, I would encourage you to vape because vaping is not dangerous to others. If you choose to vape, I would strongly recommend you shop around and buy from a local store instead of buying online.

As a nonsmoker, I prefer being around those who vape because it smells better. Vaping does not affect secondhand smokers.

Two websites that speak of vaping are:

http://www.ecassoc.org
http://www.fda.gov

The people who work at the electronic cigarette association set standards. For a business to be part of the association, they must follow the standards of the association.

The people who work for the Food and Drug Administration test prescription drugs, over-the-counter drugs, and take complaints and compliments.

Have you researched vaping?

___ Yes ___ No

Have you decided that vaping is good or bad?

___ Good ___ Bad ___ Maybe ___ Don't Know

Why?_____

_____

_____

Do you vape?

___ Yes ___ No

Why?_____

_____

_____

Will you start using electronic smoking devices?

    ___ Yes   ___ No   ___ Maybe   ___ Don't Know

Why?_____

_____

_____

If you are a smoker, do you want to vape instead?

    ___ Yes   ___ No   ___ Maybe   ___ Don't Know

Why?_____

_____

_____

Are you an ex-smoker?

    ___ Yes   ___ No

Are you a nonsmoker (someone who has never smoked in their life)?

    ___ Yes   ___ No

    Here are examples of closeness for the next few questions. If you are a smoker, answer the question regarding an ex-smoker or nonsmoker. If you are an ex-smoker or nonsmoker, answer the question regarding a smoker.

At what level do you feel comfortable being friends with a smoker, ex-smoker or nonsmoker?

    ___ Telephone friends
    ___ Friends that meet in neutral places like a restaurant, mall, school, or bus station
    ___ Online friends/Internet friends
    ___ Friends that visit at each other's houses

Why do you feel that way?

_____

_____

_____

_____

If you are a nonsmoker or ex-smoker, would you consider marrying a smoker?

___ Yes ___ No ___ Maybe ___ Don't Know

Why or why not?_____

_____

_____

_____

How physically close to a smoker would you feel comfortable?

_____

_____

_____

Local Transportation

(YOU CAN CHOOSE MORE THAN ONE WAY TO TRAVEL AROUND TOWN!)

Would you want to walk?

___ Yes ___ No ___ Sometimes
___ Maybe ___ Don't Know

If yes, how many blocks or miles can you walk?

____ Miles
____ Blocks

Where would you want to walk to?

_____

_____

_____

Would you consider riding a bike?

___ Yes ___ No ___ Sometimes
___ Maybe ___ Don't Know

If yes, how many blocks or miles can you bicycle?

____ Miles
____ Blocks

Where would you bicycle to?

_____

_____

_____

If no, maybe, or don't know, why would you not want to bicycle?

_____

_____

_____

Are there any other forms of transportation you are willing to use?

　　___ Yes　___ No　___ Maybe　___ Don't Know

If yes, what are they?

_____

_____

_____

Disability Van
(Also Called Paratransit or Dial-a-Ride)

The disability van is a service offered to people who have severe enough disabilities that riding the city bus is too dangerous or difficult. You must apply and be eligible to ride the disability van. It is a door-to-door service. Passengers must schedule their rides in advance.

The county that you live in will determine how far in advance you must schedule your ride. (For example, Spokane County requires 2-7 days advance notice.)

Do you want to apply to ride the disability van?

    ___ Yes   ___ No   ___ Maybe   ___ Don't Know

Why or why not?_____

_____

_____

_____

When do you need to ride? Here is a list. (Check all that apply for the disability van.)

    ___ Day
    ___ Night
    ___ Fall
    ___ Winter
    ___ Spring
    ___ Summer
    ___ Weekends
    ___ Go to unfamiliar areas
    ___ During the holidays that public transportation observes

Do you need a personal care attendant?

___ Yes   ___ No   ___ Sometimes   ___ Don't Know

City Bus

Riding the city bus involves being around everyone!

The city bus is quicker than the disability van in getting you where you want to go. It is not a door-to-door service.

Are you interested in riding the city buses?

___ Yes ___ No

Why or why not?_____

_____

_____

Are you interested in learning *how* to ride the city buses?

___ Yes ___ No

Why or why not?_____

_____

_____

Do you know any "safety tips" when riding the city bus?

___ Yes ___ No

If yes, what are *your safety tips* that you use to keep yourself safe on the city bus?

_____

_____

_____

_____

Do you need help in knowing how to keep yourself safe when riding the city bus?

___ Yes ___ No

If yes, who do you want to teach you safety tips for riding the city bus?

_____

_____

Driving

The most independent way to get around is by driving, but it is also the *most expensive* way to travel. Some people don't drive due to disability or because they broke the law.

Do you want to drive?

___ Yes   ___ No   ___ Not Sure

If you're not sure, what do you need to find out so you can decide?

_____

_____

_____

If yes, how much money do you need to save to buy a car?

$ _____

How much money would you be willing to spend on fixing a car?

$ _____

How much money can you afford to budget every paycheck for gas, car insurance, and money for when your car needs to be repaired?

$ _____

Would you consider carpooling?

___ Yes   ___ No   ___ Sometimes
___ Maybe   ___ Don't Know

Who would you carpool with? (Examples of this would be riding with smokers, religious people, co-workers, or only with people you know.)

_____

_____

_____

At what age do you think *you will have enough maturity* to drive?

    _____ Years Old

What protection barriers would you want to be put in place to be a safe driver? (An example, who will you give your keys to *before* you start drinking alcohol, *if* you *choose* to drink alcohol?)

_____

_____

_____

_____

Who would you feel safe driving you home if you have been drinking alcohol?

_____

_____

Do you know what driving accommodations are?

    ___ Yes ___ No

If yes, what are they?

_____

_____

_____

(Accommodations need to be specific to an individual's disability.)

Do you need any driving accommodations?

___ Yes ___ No

If yes, what?

_____

_____

_____

Employment

What was your dream job as a child?

_____

_____

_____

What was your dream job as a teenager?

_____

_____

_____

As a teenager, did you have a job?

___ Yes ___ No

If yes, how many? _____

If yes, where did you work? _____

_____

As an adult, how many hours do you think you can comfortably work a day?

_____ Hours

As an adult, how many dollars are you willing to accept as your lowest amount of pay per hour?

$ _____

Would you *enjoy* a job?

___ Yes ___ No

Do you enjoy working on or with machines?

    ___ Yes ___ No

If yes, what kind of machines?

_____

_____

_____

Do you enjoy doing physical labor?

    ___ Yes ___ No

If yes, what kind of physical labor?

_____

_____

_____

Do you enjoy doing office work such as answering phones, typing on the computer, filing, and more?

    ___ Yes ___ No

If yes, how many words can you type a minute? _____

Do you enjoy doing data entry and working with different computer programs?

    ___ Yes ___ No

Do you enjoy fixing computers when they break?

    ___ Yes ___ No

Do you enjoy doing restaurant work which includes host/hostess, waiter/waitress, dishwasher, or cook?

___ Yes ___ No

Do you enjoy planting seeds or picking plants?

___ Yes ___ No

If yes, what kind of plants?

_____

_____

_____

Do you enjoy making clothes?

___ Yes ___ No

If yes, what kind of clothes?

_____

_____

_____

Do you enjoy engineering?

___ Yes ___ No

If yes, what kind of engineering?

_____

_____

_____

Do you enjoy aeronautics?

    ___ Yes ___ No

If yes, what kind of aeronautics?

_____

_____

_____

Do you enjoy working with the public?

    ___ Yes ___ No

Do you enjoy working with co-workers?

    ___ Yes ___ No

Do you enjoy working with other people?

    ___ Yes ___ No

Do you enjoy working alone?

    ___ Yes ___ No

    This next set of questions is related to what **you are good at doing**! *Nobody is good at everything!*

Are you good at working with machines?

    ___ Yes ___ No

What kind of machines?

_____

_____

_____

Are you good at doing physical labor?

    ___ Yes ___ No

What kind of physical labor?

_____

_____

_____

Are you good at doing office work such as answering phones, typing on the computer, filing, and more?

    ___ Yes ___ No

Are you good at doing data entry and working with different computer programs?

    ___ Yes ___ No

Are you good at fixing computers when they break?

    ___ Yes ___ No

Are you good at restaurant work which includes host/hostess, waiter/waitress, a dishwasher, or a cook?

    ___ Yes ___ No

Are you good at planting seeds or picking plants?

    ___ Yes ___ No

Are you good at making clothes?

    ___ Yes ___ No

Are you good at engineering?

    ___ Yes ___ No

Are you good at aeronautics?

___ Yes ___ No

Are you good at working with the public?

___ Yes ___ No

Are you good at working with co-workers?

___ Yes ___ No

Are you good at working by yourself when other people are around you?

___ Yes ___ No

Are you good at working alone when no one is around?

___ Yes ___ No ___ Sometimes
___ Kind Of ___ Don't Know

How to Narrow Down Your Choice of Jobs

1) You can begin to narrow your choices by eliminating jobs that you don't enjoy and that you are not good at.
2) It would be smart to research jobs that you enjoy and that you are good at.
3) The next step would be to find the right amount of pay you are willing to accept.
4) Does the job you want to do require more education? If so, see the chapter on college.

Some jobs, like singing in a band, don't pay a lot of money but *might be* worth it. Another type of job that doesn't pay a lot are jobs at religious organizations. However, the spiritual rewards might be worth it!

Agencies that can help people find work:

- Developmental Disabilities Administration (DDA)
- Department of Vocational Rehabilitation (DVR)
- Services for the Blind

Is your best way/style of learning "On the Job Training?"

___ Yes ___ No

Are there any agencies that will help you find a job that you enjoy doing?

___ Yes ___ No

What are the names of the agencies that could help you get the job of your dreams?

_____

_____

_____

If you are interested in earning a lot of money, a smart idea would be to consider going to college!

College

You have a better chance of getting a higher paying job if you go to college! The higher the college degree, the better paying job you should be able to get.

There are jobs you can get that you do not have to go to college for. However, if you go to college to get more skills, you have a better chance of getting a raise or a promotion at work! Some employers will not hire you unless you have a college degree.

In thinking about going to college ask yourself these questions:

How much money do you need to make a month at a future job?

$_____

How much money do you want to make a month at a future job?

$_____

(When researching jobs, the pay may be presented as "$40K w/ med." This translates into earning $40,000 a year plus medical benefit. They assume you understand that any dollar amount they give means yearly amounts, not by the month, week, day, or hour unless specified.)

For all jobs you would enjoy and be good at, research them to find out if going to college is required for the job.

If going to college is required for some of these jobs, what are the required classes?

_____

_____

_____

What kind of degree do you need?

    ___ Less than 2 years   ___ 2 year (AA)   ___ 4 year (BA)
    ___ 6 year (MA)   ___ 8 year (PhD)   ___ Longer

In what area of study are you getting your college degree?

_____

_____

_____

What is your reason for going to college? Is it to get a job?

    ___ Yes ___ No

    If yes, there are grants, scholarships, loans, and work study programs specific to paying for college. If you have a disability, DVR, DDA, or Services for the Blind *might be* able to help you find money to pay for college or will pay for your classes if you show them that you are serious about going to work.

    If you are not going to college for employment reasons, look at different ways for college to be paid for, such as family, other scholarships, or government programs.

How are you going to pay for college?

_____

_____

_____

Do you want to go to college?

    ___ Yes ___ No

If yes, for what degree and for how long? If no, what are your plans for work?

_____

_____

_____

_____

Wants

Choosing a Cell Phone Company

Strong recommendation: Take someone from your support team with you to a cell phone store. **Don't sign** any papers without someone you trust reading the paperwork and saying, "It is **safe to sign!**"

Cell phone terms and definitions:

"Anytime minutes" means you pay a set amount of money each month for that number of minutes for specific hours of the day, and certain days of the week. **Every cell phone company is different** regarding anytime minutes and the days of the week. For example, anytime minutes could be 7:00 a.m. – 7:00 p.m. or it could be 9:00 a.m. – 9:00 p.m. Ask the salesperson!

"Monthly plan" means how much you pay each month for the service of your choice.

"Kickbacks" means the way cell phone companies (and other businesses) reward their customers for recommending their company to new customers.

Research all cell phone companies to see which one meets your needs and meets your price range!

Do you want a cell phone?

___ Yes   ___ No

Why or why not?_____

_____

_____

Do you think that you need a cell phone?

___ Yes   ___ No

Why or why not?_____

_____

_____

Cell Phone Prices

Would you give up something (i.e. cable) to pay for a cell phone?

    ___ Yes   ___ No

How would you pay your cell phone bill every month?

_____

_____

_____

    Most or all cell phone companies require you to have a credit card or debit card to pay your bill over the phone or over the internet. If you would rather pay with check or money order, ask the company if that's okay.

    Sometimes cell phone companies change the plans they offer. You need to be on a plan until your contract is over. When the contract is over, it's up to the cell phone company to ask you about keeping or changing your plan, or they might automatically update your plan to another plan with or without your permission. The updated plan will probably cost more and would probably be close to your current plan!

    Some people choose to have a work cell phone and a personal cell phone. If you have two cell phones, you will need a contract for each phone number.

What is your most comfortable way of communicating with a cell phone company? Do you need/want to talk to a live customer service representative on the telephone?

___ Yes ___ No

Do you need/want to use an automated telephone system?

___ Yes ___ No

Do you have a computer?

___ Yes ___ No

If so, do you know how to use the internet to pay the bill?

___ Yes ___ No

If so, would you consider paying your bill online?

___ Yes ___ No

Why or why not?_____

_____

_____

If you answered yes to all three questions, would you feel safe doing your business over the internet?

___ Yes ___ No

Why or why not?_____

_____

_____

Do you have the time to go to the store?

___ Yes ___ No

If you want to go to the store, where are the cell phone stores closest to you?

_____

_____

_____

Your Job Might Limit Your Choices!

Do you have a job?

___ Yes ___ No

Does your job require the employees to have a cell phone?

___ Yes ___ No

Does your place of work buy cell phones for its employees?

___ Yes ___ No

If the employer buys and pays for the employee's cell phone, the employer gets to choose the cell phone company and the plan; not you, unless the employer says the employee can!

If you use your cell phone for work, will your boss pay for part of your cell phone bill?

___ Yes ___ No

If not and you want a cell phone, will you tell your boss to give you a cell phone for work?

___ Yes ___ No

If they will, how much will they pay a month?

_____% or $_____

If yes, do you get to choose your cell phone company?

___ Yes ___ No ___ Don't Know

If you don't know, how will you find out?

_____

_____

_____

How many hours are you home to use your landline phone?

_____ Hours

If you think you need a cell phone, do you also need a home phone?

___ Yes ___ No

Why or why not? _____

_____

_____

What are your responsibilities to your family that would cause you to need a cell phone (children or other adults)?

_____

_____

_____

What is your reason for getting a cell phone?

_____

_____

_____

Are there any cell phone companies that will accommodate your disability?

    ___ Yes   ___ No   ___ Don't Know

If you don't know, how will you find out?

_____

_____

_____

Do any of the cell phone companies offer people with disabilities financial discounts?

    ___ Yes   ___ No   ___ Don't Know

If you don't know, how will you find out?

_____

_____

_____

Do the cell phone companies require proof of disability(ies) to get the discount?

    ___ Yes   ___ No

Do any of the cell phone companies offer specials for college students?

    ___ Yes   ___ No   ___ Don't Know

If you don't know, how will you find out?

_____

_____

_____

Do any of the cell phone companies offer military personnel specials?

___ Yes   ___ No   ___ Don't Know

If you don't know, how will you find out?

_____

_____

_____

How important do you think it is to get insurance on a cell phone? (Check your answer.)

___ Very Important
___ Somewhat Important
___ Not Important
___ Don't Know

(Ask people close to you the reason for having insurance on a cell phone if you don't know anything about insurance.)

Where do you call or receive calls from? Think about where your family and friends are located in the world.

Do you need any international minutes on your plan?

___ Yes   ___ No

If yes, how many international minutes do you need each month?

_____ Minutes

Do you need national minutes on your plan? (National minutes means all over the USA.)

___ Yes   ___ No   ___ Maybe   ___ Don't Know

If yes, how many national minutes do you need each month?

_____ Minutes

Do you need any regional minutes on your plan? (Regional depends on the state and city you are in and each cell phone company has different regional areas they cover.)

___ Yes ___ No ___ Maybe ___ Don't Know

If yes, how many regional minutes do you need each month?

_____ Minutes

Do you need any local minutes on your plan?

___ Yes ___ No ___ Maybe ___ Don't Know

If yes, how many local minutes do you need each month?

_____ Minutes

Something to think about: Do you really need a home phone if you have a cell phone?

Out of Town Traveling

Make a few copies of this traveling chapter. Each copy is for a different trip.

Where do you need to travel?

_____

_____

_____

Where do you want to travel? (List all places that you are thinking of traveling to.)

_____

_____

_____

Where do you plan on going?

_____

_____

_____

List the positives about each place you need or want to travel to.

_____

_____

_____

List the negatives about each place you need or want to travel to.

_____
_____
_____

How many positives and how many negatives are there for each place you need or want to travel to?

_____
_____
_____

Where is the final place you have chosen to travel to? (Choose one place!)

_____

Be specific when answering your support team's questions!

What month(s) and day(s) are you available for traveling?

_____
_____

What month, day, and year have you chosen to leave town?

_____
_____

What month, day, and year are you coming back?

_____
_____

Are you going to travel with other people?

___ Yes ___ No ___ Maybe ___ Don't Know

How many people are you traveling with? _____

Who are they?

_____

_____

_____

What are the positives of each person you are considering traveling with?

_____

_____

_____

_____

What are the negatives of each person you are considering traveling with?

_____

_____

_____

_____

How much money do you need to save for your trip?

$_____

How much do you have saved now?

$_____

How much money do you still need to save?

$_____

Do you want to get a credit card for traveling out of town?

___ Yes   ___ No   ___ Maybe

Why or why not or what do you need to find out?

_____

_____

_____

Do you know how to use traveler's checks?

___ Yes   ___ No

Do you have extra money for "the fun stuff" such as postcards and other souvenirs?

___ Yes   ___ No

How much "extra money" do you want to take with you total?

$_____

Do you have extra money to put in an emergency fund that you can take with you? (An emergency fund is money saved that you don't plan on spending, unless you have to.)

___ Yes   ___ No

If you are a spiritual person and you will be traveling alone, talk to one close male and one close female friend who share your spiritual values so you can be held accountable to your spiritual values while you are away from the people you know.

If you are recovering from an addiction(s), you will need and want to be held accountable by talking to others recovering from the same addiction(s). Talk to one male and one female who are recovering from the same addiction(s) that you are. These people should be able to help you stick to your religious and/or recovery beliefs when you are traveling.

What is the crime rate in the city and state you are going to?

_____

_____

What kind of crime(s) happen most often in the city you are visiting?

_____

_____

Are the people friendly where you're going?

    ___ Yes ___ No ___ Don't Know

Do people in that town make eye contact?

    ___ Yes ___ No ___ Don't Know

When it comes to purchasing travel accommodations and transportation, shop around. If you have time, look for discount prices for traveling and hotel/motel. In restaurants, share the cost of meals by sharing a meal. Share a hotel/motel room together. Travel around the city together and share the cost of the taxicabs, rent-a-car, or the gas in somebody's personal vehicle. Share the cost of transportation to the city you are traveling to. For example, is there a buy two tickets for the price of one sale?

How do you plan on getting to the city and state you are visiting? (Check the ONE that applies.)

    ___ Airplane
    ___ Greyhound Bus
    ___ Train
    ___ Driving Your Own Car

Other: _____

How are you paying to get there? (Check all that apply.)

    ___ Pay in Person
    ___ Pay over the Phone
    ___ Pay over the Internet
    ___ Pay with Cash
    ___ Pay with Travelers Check
    ___ Pay with Credit Card
    ___ Pay with Debit Card
    ___ Pay through PayPal
    ___ Pay with Check

    Share cost (example, buy one, get the second ticket free).

How many people can you share the transportation cost with?

_____

How do you plan on getting around this place? (Check all that apply.)

    ___ Disability Van
    ___ City Bus
    ___ Driving your own car
    ___ Rent-a-car
    ___ Taxicab

Other: _____

How do you plan on paying for your transportation in the town you are in? (Check all that apply.)

    ___ Share the cost
    ___ Pay with Cash
    ___ Pay with Traveler's Check
    ___ Pay with Debit Card
    ___ Pay with Credit Card
    ___ Pay with Money Order
    ___ Pay with Check
    ___ Riding around with a friend/family member who lives in the town you are visiting

If you are going to share the cost, how many people are you going to share the cost with?_____

If it takes you a couple of days until you do get there, where will you stay until you get there? Be specific with names of the hotel/motel and/or friends, the addresses, phone numbers, and email addresses.

_____

_____

_____

_____

Where will you be staying when you arrive in town? (Check all that apply.)

    ___ Hotel/Motel   ___ Family   ___ Friends

Will you be sharing the shelter cost with anyone?

    ___ Yes   ___ No

How many people will be sharing the shelter cost? _____

How much money will your share of the shelter cost be per night?

$_____

If you stay in a hotel/motel, does your room have a kitchenette?

___ Yes ___ No ___ Don't Know

Are you going to buy groceries?

___ Yes ___ No

If your room has a kitchenette, are you going to cook food in the kitchenette?

___ Yes ___ No ___ Sometimes

Are you going to eat out at restaurants?

___ Yes ___ No ___ Sometimes

How many of you will be sharing one plate of food? _____

When you split a large meal, will you be splitting the cost among all the people who eat that meal?

___ Yes ___ No

Will you be eating at family members' or friends' houses?

___ Yes ___ No

If eating at a family member's or friend's house, will you be helping them with the cost of the food?

___ Yes ___ No

(Some family and friends will not accept money for food when you are staying in their home, others will.)

Is this a planned trip?

    ___ Yes   ___ No

Is this an emergency trip? (Ex., family emergency)

    ___ Yes   ___ No

If this is an emergency trip and you have a job, put in a "leave of absence."

If you don't or won't do financial business over the internet, consider asking for another person's help. For example, a man I know went to Kansas. He asked his sister to buy the ticket over the internet and to get a receipt. When she showed her brother the receipt, he paid his sister back. It was as if he had bought the ticket himself; but the price was cheaper over the internet than on the phone or in person. (His sister bought it at the cheapest rate.)

When flying, find someone to take you to the airport or take public transportation. If you park at the airport during your trip, you will be charged for *every hour* your car is parked there.

When planning your trip, list the things that need to be done and check things off as they get done:

    ___ Put a hold on the mail
    ___ Put a hold on the newspaper
    ___ Find someone to feed the pets
    ___ Find someone to water the plants
    ___ Find someone to stay at your house while you are on vacation!

Check to see if you have bought and packed all your necessities for your trip. Check your list twice, once for being bought and a second time for being packed.

Cross off each thing as it gets done:

    ___ Prescription medications
    ___ Personal Hygiene (hairbrush, toothbrush, toothpaste, mouthwash, floss)
    ___ Cell Phone or phone card
    ___ Cell Phone Charger
    ___ Traveler's Checks
    ___ Laptop Computer
    ___ Your ticket (bus, airplane, train, etc.)

Do you have a child or children going with you?

    ___ Yes ___ No

How many children? _____

Make a list of every child's needs and wants. As you put each thing in your suitcase for your children, cross it off the list so you know it's packed just like your stuff is packed.

Now, you are ready to go. You might want to make a second list for your return trip. (Things to buy and pack.)

Looking for a Close Relationship

(Make copies of this chapter. Use it for each significant relationship.)

What are your hobbies?

_____

_____

_____

What are the other person's hobbies?

_____

_____

_____

What hobbies do the two of you have in common?

_____

_____

_____

What hobbies do the two of you have that are different?

_____

_____

_____

Does the other person respect your hobbies?

___ Yes ___ No

Do you respect the other person's hobbies?

___ Yes ___ No

How do the two of you respect each individual's hobbies?

_____

_____

_____

Can the other person accept all of your bad habits?

___ Yes ___ No

Can you accept all of the other person's bad habits?

___ Yes ___ No

How do you cope with their bad habits?

_____

_____

_____

How do they cope with your bad habits?

_____

_____

_____

How long would you want to know someone before you would feel comfortable being touched by the other person?

_____

What kind of touch? (Please specify the time)

    ___ Holding hands: How long? _____
    ___ Hugging: How long? _____
    ___ Kissing: How long? _____
    ___ Nuzzling nose to nose: How long? _____

How long would you need to know someone before you would "feel safe" giving a person your phone number?

    ___ Days   ___ Weeks   ___ Months   ___ Years

What would make you "feel safe" about giving a person your phone number?

_____

_____

_____

How long would you need to know someone before you would "feel safe" giving a person your email address?

    ___ Days   ___ Weeks   ___ Months   ___ Years

What would make you "feel safe" about giving that person your email address?

_____

_____

_____

How long would you need to know someone before you would "feel safe" giving someone (especially someone who has a crush on you) your physical address?

___ Days ___ Weeks ___ Months ___ Years

What would make you "feel safe" about giving that person your physical address?

_____

_____

_____

Do you have children?

___ Yes ___ No

Do you want to have children?

___ Yes ___ No

Why or why not?_____

_____

_____

Dating, living together, and marrying on the rebound is usually bad.

Raising Children

Do you ever want to have children?

    ___ Yes ___ No

Why or why not?_____

_____

_____

Have you ever taken care of an animal(s)/pet(s)?

    ___ Yes ___ No

If so, what kind of animal(s)/pet(s)?

_____

Do you have younger brothers or sisters?

    ___ Yes ___ No

If you do, did you ever take care of them?

    ___ Yes ___ No

Have you ever taken care of other younger relatives, such as nieces, nephews, or cousins?

    ___ Yes ___ No

Have you ever taken any babysitting or childcare classes?

    ___ Yes ___ No

Have you ever done childcare for the neighborhood or for a religious organization?

    ___ Yes ___ No

Have you ever taken any parenting classes?

    ___ Yes   ___ No

How do you handle stress in your day-to-day life?

_____

_____

_____

How do you handle the stress of things changing every day?

_____

_____

_____

How do you think you would handle those same stressful situations with a child or children living with you?

_____

_____

_____

How do you *think* you would handle *changes* with a child as they grow and mature? (Changes could be the way a child needs to be disciplined as they get older.)

_____

_____

_____

Do you want to be a natural parent?

    ___ Yes ___ No

Why or why not?_____

_____

_____

Do you want to be a stepparent?

    ___ Yes ___ No

Why or why not?_____

_____

_____

Do you want to be part of a blended family?

    ___ Yes ___ No

Why or why not?_____

_____

_____

Do you want to live with someone who has children?

    ___ Yes ___ No

Why or why not?_____

_____

_____

There are different kinds of children who are up for adoption. They are different by age, the country they were born in, the reason they are up for adoption, and the type of adoption. Depending on your family, cultural and ethnic background, adoption may or may not be a good idea.

There are open adoptions, closed adoptions, relative adoptions, private adoptions, public adoptions, state-to-state adoptions, and international adoptions.

"Open adoption" means allowing the child or children to stay in contact with their birth parents in some way.

"Closed adoption" means the child or children have no contact with the birth parents and/or may not even know who their birth parents are.

Do you want to adopt a child or children?

___ Yes ___ No

Why or why not?_____

_____

_____

If yes, what age group are you looking at adopting?

_____

What gender are you looking at adopting?

___ Male ___ Female

Do you want to adopt a child in the USA?

___ Yes ___ No ___ Doesn't Matter

Do you want to adopt a child outside the USA?

___ Yes ___ No ___ Doesn't Matter

Is there a child in your extended family that some other adult in your family cannot take care of?

___ Yes ___ No

If there is a child in your extended family that the parents can't raise, would you want to adopt that child to keep them in the family?

___ Yes ___ No

Why or why not?_____

_____

_____

Would you want to adopt if it was going to be an open adoption?

___ Yes ___ No

Why or why not?_____

_____

_____

Would you want to adopt if it was going to be a closed adoption?

___ Yes ___ No

Why or why not?_____

_____

_____

Do you want to be a guardian of a child?

___ Yes ___ No

You can be a foster parent without adopting! Foster parents take children in temporarily during the time a judge says the parents can't take care of their children. Foster parents see children come and go all the time, sometimes even in the middle of the night and/or without letting them know ahead of time!

Foster parents are employed by the state they live in. Being a foster parent is a 24 hour a day, 7 day a week job. A foster parent is not allowed to get regular childcare. When the foster parent needs some time for themselves, the foster parent <u>must find</u> another <u>licensed foster care family, with the same criteria</u> as them.

Do you want to be a foster parent?

    ___ Yes   ___ No

If yes, what kind of children? (Check all that apply.)

    ___ Children or teenagers who have broken the law.
    ___ Children or teenagers who are delayed.
    ___ Children or teenagers who are disabled.
    ___ Children or teenagers who have a mental illness.
    ___ Children or teenagers who are orphans.
    ___ Children or teenagers who have been abused.
    ___ Children or teenagers who have emotional issues.
    ___ Children or teenagers who have chemical dependency problems.

What age? (Check all that apply.)

    ___ Infants
    ___ Toddlers
    ___ Preschoolers
    ___ Elementary children
    ___ Younger teenagers
    ___ Older teenagers

When it's time to find a childcare provider to take a break, *how* will you choose someone *who is safe* to watch your *own* child(ren)?

_____

_____

_____

How much do you need to pay the childcare provider?

$_____

Whose house will your child(ren) stay at? (Check answer.)

___ Child(ren)'s house   ___ Sitter's house

How long will you be out?

_____

Do you have the money to pay *both* the childcare provider and to pay for your outing?

___ Yes   ___ No

Resources for the Disability Community

There are many types of resources for the disability community.

Public transportation helps everyone get around who don't drive. Public transportation also helps people save money!

There are many kinds of assistant living homes to choose from. There are adult family homes, group homes, CCF's, care centers, and independent living centers to learn independent living skills.

Other resources can help people gain employment. Resources could be Developmental Disabilities Administration (DDA), Division of Vocational Rehabilitation (DVR), or Services for the Blind; however, there are others.

A credit card is another type of resource. It can be used if you need to buy something or put something on hold over the phone. However, one credit card is all you need! The reason is, the more credit cards a person has, the easier it is to go into debt.

Not only do you owe the money that you spent buying something using the credit card, you will also have to pay it back plus interest. Paying interest when you don't have to is **bad for you** *financially*!

When considering buying a "big purchase," take someone from your support team with you to verify if the purchase is worth the price. There's a <u>lower chance</u> of being taken advantage of and <u>once you learn to price things correctly</u>, you won't need as much assistance. You may need to ask someone to take you home in their car/truck when you buy a large item so you can get it home.

If a person has trouble managing money and they receive money from Social Security Administration, Social Security Administration might insist that you have "representative protective payee."

"Representative protective payee" is a phrase used only by

Social Security Administration for a person who takes care of their client's money. The person who has the disability can usually choose who their payee is. However, Social Security Administration *must* approve of the person the client chooses. The payee can only manage government money!

A trustee takes care of all other financial resources. (Ask your support team if you need help understanding the difference between a representative protective payee and a trustee.) A trustee takes care of a "trust." A "trust" can be for an education, extraordinary medical expenses, work accommodations, or other reasons

If you want to live alone and struggle with personal care tasks and housekeeping, there are programs that can help take care of those needs. One is COPES and the other is Personal Care Medicaid. These programs help people with things they are unable to do for themselves.

The rules for these programs depend on the state you live in. (You *must have* a certain number of personal care tasks to be eligible for either service.) If you get too much money, you can pay for the services yourself.

Family and friends are resources. They can help with any transportation and housework you need if you don't have enough hours. The way the government works, they might say you are eligible for less hours than you really need.

Do you want to see if your family or friends want or can assist you sometimes?

    ___ Yes   ___ No   ___ Maybe

Don't take advantage of your family or your friends! (It's not considered "taking advantage" *when* that person *is going to the same place you* are or the same direction you are at the same time.)

Every state has a large resource directory to find all the resources you need in your area. The number to dial is 211.

There are resources for getting and maintaining the correct weight, managing money, assertiveness training, etc.

Assertiveness training will be your *best defense against* someone taking advantage of you because you'll have the skills you need to prevent someone from taking advantage of you and the skills to ask for what you need! If you learn to be assertive, life will be easier and safer.

The last two resources are self-advocacy and group advocacy if you disagree with any decision about services, such as being denied a service.

When all the people with disabilities are being denied for the same reason, it is time to go talk to the politicians and fight for all the people with disabilities and their rights! (This works for any group of people who are being treated disrespectfully or being denied something that other people get.)

"Self-advocacy" is an individual fighting to get something they are entitled to and need but have been denied! These would be services the law already has in place, but an individual person has been denied. It could also be an individual fighting to get rid of a service/benefit they are eligible for.

"Group advocacy" is a group of people fighting for their rights to be treated equal, to have the same rights everyone does. It could be fighting for things that lawmakers might think we don't need. So, as a group of people, they stand up together and tell the politicians what they need!

Here are some questions to ask yourself when you consider using resources for the disability community.

How do you travel around town?

    ___ Disability Van
    ___ City Bus
    ___ Personal Car
    ___ Bicycle
    ___ Walking

What is your choice of housing?

    ___ Assisted Living
    ___ Renting a Room
    ___ Living Alone

If you want to live alone, do you need help with personal care or managing your money?

    ___ Yes ___ No ___ Maybe
    ___ Sometimes ___ Don't Know

Do you need help to get a job or maintain your job?

    ___ Yes ___ No ___ Maybe
    ___ Sometimes ___ Don't Know

If so, what organization helps you?

_____

_____

_____

Do you want or need assistance with pricing "big purchase" items?

    ___ Yes ___ No ___ Maybe
    ___ Sometimes ___ Don't Know

Can you be assertive in stating your opinions?

    ___ Yes ___ No ___ Maybe
    ___ Sometimes ___ Don't Know

Can you comfortably ask for what you need and want?

    ___ Yes ___ No ___ Maybe
    ___ Sometimes ___ Don't Know

Do you know where to go if you are denied services you need to maintain your independence?

___ Yes   ___ No

If so, where will you go if you are denied services?

_____

_____

_____

If not, what do you need to do to find out where you can go if you are denied services?

_____

_____

_____

Who are your natural supports? (A natural support of anyone around you who helps you who is not getting paid to help you.)

_____

_____

_____

The Challenges of Living on Your Own

Here are some words and simple definitions.

Interests: Things people enjoy. Everyone's interests are different.

Hobbies: Things and activities people spend their energy, money, and time on. Hobbies can be done with someone else or by yourself.

Goals: Things you want to achieve or accomplish in the short and long run.

Support Groups: Places you go to when you want and/or need to stop addictions. The people in these groups make good community friends and phone friends. However, it might not be safe to give your physical address to people in addiction type support groups.

Other types of Support Groups: This kind of support group is where people share the same kind of disability. I would strongly recommend knowing a person for one year before giving them your physical address.

Support Team: *All* of your professional and personal support groups put together. This includes your power of attorney/guardian, close friends, people from your place of worship, family members you choose, advocates, political friends, and social service places.

If you want to move out on your own, here are some safety tips to think about!

A) Know yourself. Know your boundaries when looking to be a roommate or looking for a roommate. Know yourself well enough to know if you can live happily with the person you just met to be their roommate.

B) Find out what your best way of communicating with others is whether that is by talking, writing, or using a computer to speak for you, etc. Set your boundaries around your property, your home, time that people are allowed to call you, and when they are allowed to come to your house.

Don't try to be friends with everyone; you won't have enough time for yourself and you will probably burn out!

Plan your days by what you *have to do*. First, this would include going to your doctor appointments, school or work, and taking care of yourself and family (including children). Taking care of yourself might be going out on a date or out with your significant other. Taking care of your child(ren) is finding someone *you trust* to watch your child(ren) when you go out. Who will keep your child(ren) healthy, have the child(ren) obey *your* rules, and help the child(ren) do their schoolwork?

You need to make time for calling people on the phone. These calls could be to the doctors, child's schoolteacher, disability van service, your support team, etc.

If you run short on time, it may be worth the financial investment to get a cell phone. If you drive, get a Bluetooth for your cell phone! A cell phone is also worth having for long distance calls or if you need to call for a ride. Using a phone while traveling as a passenger is considered "good time management!"

Things you can do as a passenger on a disability van, city bus, or as a passenger in a car include calling your friends, making doctor's appointments for the family, writing a grocery list, doing homework, or do work that you have to take home from work.

Other members of the household can contribute by working and paying bills or doing other things such as chores around the house.

When everyone does their part, the family has time to be together!

These are everyday necessities:
- Take care of personal hygiene
- Take your medicines

- Eat at least 3 big meals a day, or 5-6 small ones a day, or any mix of big and small meals. (This will usually include cooking, at other times eating at someone's house, and other times eating out.)
- Take time to sleep

All your planning should be done in seven-day weekly periods of time.

Is Guardianship Good or Bad?

Advocates, different kinds of powers of attorney, trustees, advanced directives, wills, or a living will are <u>*all less restrictive options*</u> to keep your health protected health-wise and without having a guardian.

(If you want or need to know what the above words mean, ask a lawyer or the most knowledgeable person on your support team.)

Do you want a medical advanced directive?

___ Yes ___ No ___ Maybe

Why or why not?_____

_____

_____

If you want one, do you need help to fill it out?

___ Yes ___ No

Who do you want to help you?

_____

Do you want a mental health advanced directive?

___ Yes ___ No ___ Maybe

Why or why not?_____

_____

_____

Take reasonable health precautions and take responsibility for your own actions!

Notes

About the Author

Tiffani Harvey was born with multiple physical disabilities and later acquired two more disabilities.

She graduated from high school and completed some college.

When she became an adult, her parents believed other people were using her for their political causes because her parents were never political. She always had to explain to her parents her reasons for her decisions.

She wrote *Freedom Seeking* to help you understand why you make the decisions you make and to easily answer anybody who should know why you made those decisions.

Examples of who should know are your emotionally close family, your professional team, a couple of very close friends, and anyone a professional or a trusted family member approves of.

If this book has helped you in any way, you would like to send a review, or send any other feedback, please send it to Tiffani at responsiblyindependent@yahoo.com.

www.ingramcontent.com/pod-product-compliance
Lightning Source LLC
Chambersburg PA
CBHW071852070526
44583CB00016B/1657